Rosary of Ghosts

Grant Tarbard

Indigo Dreams Publishing

First Edition: Rosary of Ghosts
First published in Great Britain in 2017 by:
Indigo Dreams Publishing Ltd
24 Forest Houses
Halwill
Beaworthy
EX21 5UU
www.indigodreams.co.uk

Grant Tarbard has asserted his right under the Copyright,
Designs and Patents Act 1988 to be identified as the author of
this work.
©2017 Grant Tarbard

ISBN 978-1-910834-47-3

British Library Cataloguing in Publication Data. A CIP record
for this book can be obtained from the British Library.

Designed and typeset in Palatino Linotype by Indigo Dreams.
Cover design by Ronnie Goodyer at Indigo Dreams
Printed and bound in Great Britain by: 4edge Ltd
www.4edge.co.uk

Papers used by Indigo Dreams are recyclable products made
from wood grown in sustainable forests following the guidance
of the Forest Stewardship Council.

For Jah

My thanks to the editors of the magazines that these poems first appeared in, most were earlier versions:

Absence first appeared in Peeking Cat; *Night Before an Operation, Broken Pinocchio, Hasten to Pasture, Blinkered Motion* and *Experiments in Smoking* first appeared in Fat Damsel; *How to Be Air* first appeared in The Lake; *Fairytale of a First Christmas, Triptych, Stranger in Bed Four* and *Stuffed Paws* first appeared in The Seventh Quarry; *Chest of Drawers, Hands Peripheral* and *Man Like You* first appeared in Your One Phone Call; *Breast Fragments* first appeared in Ginosko Literary Journal; *Here's to the End of Fading Games* first appeared in Abbreviate Journal; *Rosary of Ghosts* first appeared in The Black Light Engine Room; *Underneath the Covers* first appeared in Elbow Room; *Winter Garden* first appeared in Amaryllis Poetry; *Quicksand of Me* first appeared in Playerist; *Beneath My Blue Crippled Eye* first appeared in Degenerate Literature; *Ghost of Christmas Past* first appeared in Puff Puff Prose Poetry and a Play; *Vascular Graft* appeared in the anthology Stairs and Whispers: D/deaf and Disabled Poets Write Back (Nine Arches Press).

CONTENTS

Man Like You
to a surgeon

Torn head, all is straw,
a thunder machine
bellows in my heart.
Beneath this gown I
am a man like you.

How to Be Air

I am from nothing, a beak's whistle of cloud,
a piece of November intended to be oxygen.

What lies within the salt white rhythm of gravity?
Compartments of a feather, insubstantial as blown ash.

Imagine buoyancy with a flushed cheek,
a red faced huff of air above the light of the room,

the smoke of a terrace of spent cigarettes,
ribbons of silk spooning in the ventilation.

The problems arise when one wants to land-
will my melodramatic body come apart,

mistrusting finger joints and the arm's gristle
to tighten – snatching out at aerials on rooftops.

I latch on to the rusting shed of tobacco tins,
my grandfather's loose nails fasten me down.

Triptych

I have had three deaths,
one for each decade.

To hide them from myself
I've concealed barren pages of earth

underneath the catacomb grey floorboards,
I press my cheek to my deaths, a slow dance

with an ostrich, I taste his arid breath
eaten whole,

beyond sentiment,
dressed in clothes of darkness.

The pain from old wounds
ache like wedding white.

Night Before an Operation

Mentally, all my luggage was packed,
black bags deseed my packing-crate eyes

as I drank slowly the hours medicine,
the spider bite fed on my neck.

My pupils turned white without speech
as I burst into dust from clay and back again,

these raw materials that anticipate dissection,
a golem kneaded my shoulders.

In the night ward Vermeer's bulb
has burnt out its filament,

no longer is the evening painted
with burnished light, pitch swallowed

by a tattered jacket of black, of congealed ash
that sticks to the back of the throat.

I use Egyptian blue ink to paint my
eyes shut, and in my pyjama pocket folds

there're a hundred painted idols that keep guard
over my clay pudding until the next day.

Vascular Graft

The anaesthesiologist billows
fogs of gas as I undertook the third operation.

The surgeon bellows confidently
We'll make those veins stand up and take notice.

Stabbing at my flesh, the cannula
is a slap in the face, then a touch of sleep.

In my recovery through the windows
the lampposts leer like sickles,

my teeth and gums almost vicious with morphine.
I rest on gnawing bone in a thin lipped sneer.

Ghost of Christmas Past

Wounded, you sat unrecognisable,
the holy Virgin figurine's white blur

buried within me in a burrow of drugs.
I motioned for you to disappear, and you did

leaving a tear that blistered my cheek,
a form of stigmata that I'm not sure happened.

I remember a doctor talking about his Christmas,
home to Austria to ski and sip hot chocolate.

A blonde nurse replied she was going to Ireland
in Aron jumper to the shops amidst the ships masts

in perpetual sunset. I was the whale beached,
all cobalt flicker from my eyes absent, no lawyer,

not even allowed a call to say I wouldn't be home
for sprouts and arguments with your father.

Broken Pinocchio

To regard the invisible man
you have to close your eyes to see,

it's verboten to peek the light
tangled with ill fitting hospital gowns.

To regard the invisible man
you have to confront your own mortality,

it's vital to surrender to this sunken bed
clawing at palms soft flesh

tasting the protective circles of salt
as they pack their bags with every breath.

To regard the invisible man
you have to look past this callow parade

of Victorian caricatures of cripples.
It's hard to make your way round them,

bandaged into a bed eternally,
these bones of a broken Pinocchio.

Experiments in Smoking

The inhaling of nicotine is a curious business
within the ribcage. As raw skinned teenagers

we dabbled with brands with royal names,
far flung names, cowboy names; young man

head west. We thickened the delicate air
with our curses of smoke,

we rebel few in the nooks
curling blue fog on our tongues

in rapt expectancy of a kiss.
We nested on our whittled vapours in cold discos

where we had our rough hearts broken, *un amour de jeunesse.*
As a spectre you stir in my amputated sleep,

in the wheeze-tick of the ventilator.
My lungs never ripened to confessions with smoke.

Shallow of the Room

I found it hard to breathe
in the shallow of the room,

In the ambulance customs had quarantined
my twin tea chests of oxygen,

one's a little shrivelled and needle poked.
I have breathed as the dead breathe,

with a wheeze as shallow as a black crow
with the aid of machinery.

The ventilator's dark innards hand-crank
seconds of pretty life

as my heart bleeds red clay and ghosts
hung as Christmas decorations on all the street lamps

to the distant lapping waves of A and E.
A nurse, neck like gnarly oak,

wishes me a Merry Christmas.
My lips, rough hewn, reply with static.

Lie Upon My Bed While I Die

Lie upon my bed at my death,
we'll add our fog to Hell's gulping flames.

We are one with the deserted avenues
of a spatchcocked town,

beaks lost in pillowcase feathers
leaving behind the aftertaste of the lost parts of me.

We are a den of Fagan's thieves stealing
each little breath that rises on our chests,

that shiver of birds wrapped in a waif of leaves,
ingesting all colour to gray.

We two are the lost tribe of Israel,
floundering in the shapes of wilderness,

spectres under the stars, harlequins
of an expressionist cine-film,

we two wild flower wreaths.
Oh my, lie upon my bed while I die.

The Stranger in Bed Four

I've never seen a person dead before,
there he was, an illusory stranger
at the end of the box ward in bed four.
There was no ceremony, no clangour
of grief in a bell's wail, no dignity
'cept the vomit green curtains half hearted
draw so I could still spy the willow tree
of grey pubic hair sprouting unguarded
from the kettle spout zip of life within
death. The lack of vanity in a corpse
is understood and with his rictus grin
he sneers at the living in our goose skin,
hushing against our shell ears; *you are flawed.*
The boundary in my last breath was God.

Rosary of Ghosts

My skeleton is a ramshackle tin,
a coal burner billowing out black fumes,
my body is no place to be stuck in.

Death whispers, he sings like a violin
I won't go easy smelling Death's perfumes,
my skeleton is a ramshackle tin.

Tumbledown alleyways draped with goose skin,
a gargoyle in elaborate costumes,
my body is no place to be stuck in.

Rosary of ghosts in the bony shin
take possession of my streets playing spoons,
my skeleton is a ramshackle tin.

My heart is a feather, a bundled pin
that sticks in my chest and no more balloons,
my body is no place to be stuck in.

Spindrift pale night suspended like my sin,
made of in-flight mist in a steamed breath tomb.
My skeleton is a ramshackle tin,
my body is no place to be stuck in.

Hasten to the Pasture

Silverfish crawl around my skull.
I lay down in a pasture of stars,

kites flying in amber.
My eyes flit like moths detained in form

by drops of a street lamp's lilac in bloom,
thrown vases splintering to the tarmac

into all the wooden animals of the ark
who are lost and forever wandering.

I can hear my larynx turn to charcoal,
sunken reeds that haunt the ceiling,

my chromatic breath blows across
the florid mandala air

of this same room.
I hear the blood candied tones every night

of midnight's choir, in league with Pan,
swaddled in the grotto my of belly button.

Hymn to 2 A.M.

I'm the man with eyes larger than my head,
I hoard cobwebs in my swart window panes.
Groomed for slumber by my druggist sagging
eye lids, sleep's vocals seduce in film noir
echoes, the soil touches the sky's visage.
Dogs growl tendrils of photographic film,
overwhelming sepia, the colour
of a quiet tea. Soil on my bed stand,
a reminder of all things change. A tree
germ grows in the lineament of my
bed clothes, a blossom of amber morphine
drops recklessly on my blanched outstretched tongue,
gratefully I accept this dream. When I
sleep I don't have to suck my stomach in.

I open the door and stare at the night's
spectral heart until the night stares back. To-
night's radiance is blood drenching my hands,
immersed in a sea of holiness. In
the opaque painted corners all manner
of marvels traverse before my closed eyes.
Midnight's mail flies through the letterbox like
a cannonball, emptiness scatters in
between the notes of drifting weightlessness.
What is your name when the dark is swinging
the moon like a pocket watch? What do you
dare to do under the cloak of the moon?
Round and round she goes, a laundromat globe
cleanses with a tide of wrinkled flotsam.

Body

I have been a life without a body
sitting slumped in silence and incomplete,
tasting the fruit of bottled oxygen.
Time was a spinning Catherine Wheel in
my convalescence with fire fly bluster,
a revelation of abounding light
between the fog banks, a tempter of lost
children poised between my bones saffron wheat,
baring the dragon in hiding. And you
said you could barely feel my sweep carcass
in a conserved wind that could pluck a chick,
in a feather bed I am oxygen.
I have been a life without a body,
in my dreams I'll feed the bony monsters.

Chest of Drawers

This body is a chest of drawers,
at the centre is a Mason jar of hearts,

a stripped carcass in between feathers.
The top drawer is a mind tangled with a snarl of socks

and a labyrinth of missed sex,
kissing every part of every shadow.

This drawer is where the birth of ideas poach
in a field where light bulbs grow on the vine

of loose threads and forgotten tissues.
In the shirt drawer are hurt memories

with lollipop splints on their wings.
When the drawer is open they fly away

as paper aeroplanes scattering the seed
of my scent and the disorder of thought.

This body is a hand-me-down song
that whistles into knicker elastic.

Quicksand of Me

1.

The youthful father is long dead in me.
Withered limbs, bulging gut,
this Earth is round
my waist can prove it.

2.

That I'm still alive after hanging
my limbs out to dry
in a tubed oxygen bed
is a mistake.

3.

What happened to the boy I used to be?
I've kept anger in my pocket,
now I live in a giddy silent film.

Self Portrait, Underwater

The water I drown in is a mirror,
an awry portrait of a swollen face

collapsing in on itself,
sewing a picture book of anaemic reflections

liquefying into the linseed oil of a sickly sunset of eyes,
yielding to amber ovum.

There's debris floundering over the jamb of my waist,
gaunt tufts blow away like a gypsy dandelion

knowing there's a millimetre of oxygen
between sitting in love and posing for a death mask.

As I surface I pretend the morning is new,
painted by Holbein, jewel-like and imposing,

not rotten with my gangrenous fragrance
collapsing in on itself.

Blinkered Motion

Eyes are animals caught in a trap,
tearing, whittling away at the stem.

Two visions co-exist without knowing the other,
they permeate a drip below the root of the eye

where dreams convulse, haunting our hands
of cadmium yellow, pulling at the thread of an endless seed,

for there is no single moment of creation in our eyes,
just a stream of Ciné film on a loop, barbed as a bone.

Breast Fragments

I will stroke your breast until it fragments
with clamorous lions and foul-mouthed wasps

buzzing in formation, forming a twitching halo
around your head. Crumbs of tigers fly out

as sanguined paper streamers fixed with clots
making this butterfly heart beat for you,

virgin you, foul mouthed queen of my bleed.
I'll caress your pussy till it ejaculates a tiny house

of palpating fingertips. The lights in the trees are unprepared
for the ragged splendour of your shaking tail feather,

as black as Crawford's mascara, as soft as drowning,
alluringly blemished as an apple core.

Beneath My Blue Crippled Eye

I have a gun under my flesh,
a tear in the suit beneath my blue crippled eye,

crooked as a cherry branch. See my face?
I was raised in a cradle of stone masks

to be a lion in a crowd of cold oat daylight,
mad as a hat stand with gnarled arms of knotty oak,

but I'm as silent as a smile that breeds grins in daft faces.
I have a gun beneath my gouged flesh, stuffed with hazel twigs.

That gun is you dear,
a ballista who kills dead my lewd quarrel,

who kisses away the suicide scars on my gut,
who kisses my bad posture, my ink chutzpah.

You are Hyde, leaving your muddy footprints
on my rotting plum salivary glands.

Self Portrait, Seen From Above

This hole of eyes is filled with bare ennui,
rotate one hundred and eighty degrees
and focus out, stare stud-eyed at the room
surrounded in a cocoon of cushions,
spatchcocked on the sofa, reading aloud,
mumbling without clothes, roses wilt in tea,
guzzling skeletal air from keen nostrils.
Pores stuffed with peel and ginseng, cut dry words
from tongue, parasite nouns tear roof of mouth,
see a cosmos churning in this sour wound,
isolated, anchorite on sofa
in a silent menagerie of fish.
Being up here is a bull fight, raw strength,
plunging swords, a wounding, a death painted.

Hands Peripheral

My hands have been gutted from the inside out
into a corpse of trick questions, grotesque in colour-
veins of agate, spinel arteries, stretched skin of alabaster.

My hands are beautiful with daggers held behind my back
gently scraping at flesh in a scream of silences held in a box
beneath my tongue, salivating discreet sentences; hush-hush.

My hands are made of oak, or at least oak's echo,
I rub them and get a splinter. I'll put them in the barbecue
as an offering for good weather.

I hope my echo of hands will burn, mannequin hands,
fingerless, useless in embroidered theatre gloves,
pictorial carved aerophones that produce notes when blown.

Find me in the stalls swallowing jewels
for the coming lean times. Oh, my hands were hissing kettles,
now they've boiled to a slow sigh into the soothing wrath

of this nullity, a bagatelle of void, a permanent nihility.
My hands burn good as a witch. Oh, let my fingers be vicars
who'll tow the golden chariot when Death comes to town.

Winter Garden

The lover, wrapped up in a snug blanket,
a cocoon she'll prize apart

when paper cut sheaths of a late dawn
break over the mechanical tick of the horizon.

Her tangle of eyes compressed tight
into the sofa cushion

ignoring the pigments on the lawn,
loyal to an image of the past.

I worry about floating, how long do I sit here?
I dangle on a string of ears listening to your chest rise

and fall as if attached to a balloon, it's as if a tinker
with all his brass has made camp in your breast.

I ignore all sounds but whispers of ghosts,
thrushes singing in their winter garden.

Underneath the Covers

The night is black and draped with marigolds,
one hundred thousand shining lighthouses

raised and drowned on my crown
as distant ships are dashed on the back wall.

The nightjar's nocturnal song
pounds like typewriter keys.

In the flares of passing cars I bask,
with lucent fingertips I stretch to touch your arse.

You do not wake and I content myself
with making dirty horoscopes.

I begin counting all the little lamps
until dawn breaks its voice on the gravel

of spouting cockcrows, whistling like a red head.
The sky of butane blue rushes past the curtains

knocking over furniture like Rock & Roll.
I see through the mons Venus cranny in the covers,

I see through your cashmere night dress,
the definition is breath-taking, maybe we did it.

Stuffed Paws

No electricity dimmed our past days
in our first flat, grandiose in twilight.

We clattered through the letterbox
blind as church mice

making a racket in the wee small hours.
We thought we had the Knowledge

winding our way round the cross eyed garden,
twirling with the vague shapes of conifers,

on that patchy lawn cloaked by sunset.
I devoured your iron horse of ribs,

gulping down your photograph of the pearl sea-sway,
eating the cloud of your negligee.

And we made awkward love, fumbling
with the stuffed paws of drunks, button-eyed with night.

Fairytale of a First Christmas

Our first Christmas was a thousand miles away
with just the two of us, in love with first names.

In the morning the Sun's rays shone
through your ratty nightdress that I loved so

with tinsel threaded through,
numbed to the revolving outside of our core.

We spun around an imagined band of gold,
a plastic garland's matrimony with the TV in silence,

a chorale of smiling faces muted.
I'd like to rest my head on that memory

before all these small things become weary of us,
with you, with two heartbeats hidden away in your nest of fire.

Our last Christmas will be held together
with stretched elastic bands

covered with a liberality of faded glitter,
as cold as a struck match.

Here's to the End of Fading Games

Here's to the midnight swinging ladies
who are without stint in this mandala of patches blue

and stitches red, who put up with us rumpled men.
Here's to the ladies coughing up doves

and bumblebees tumbling down the street
as easily as dried leaves and tumbleweeds.

Here's to grease fingered men gyrating in oyster suits,
seeing sparks of dalliers on ciné reels.

Here's to she who leaves me helpless,
her scent lights glorious fires in my nostrils.

Here's to the grave diggers and the end of fading games,
poignant as a funeral dirge, silent as snow.

Here's to my blue in the face ghost,
drifting through weather stubbled bramble,

an army over the rise of stumble down needles
and loosened rose hips adorning my dowdy vintage jacket

like thorny medals, spinning the day's paint
with the blood trials of my midnight walks

made in untended daydream.
Here's to my breathless matter lying still.

Pretty Boy

Capturing the present seemed inconceivable
when young as a babe that was never meant to be.

As a child without veins I faded the skies,
forever I rose in my hospital green best

humming the waltzed melody of witches
and the scrupulous language of doctors.

In between conditions I lived in deletions,
down a supine close lay my father's brute hands

abrading my skin with cut price soap.
And I, cushion belied, was a disappointment,

a shivering choreography of breadth
regurgitated out of mother's umbilical sewing box.

Youth was an entanglement of clenches,
pinned down in confused toilets, sex in his unwanted breath.

Youth was a flushed kiss on a gymnasium mat
stretching those nervous fabrics, full of God.

The sailing hazel branches of her wet hair
exposing Aphrodite brown nipples through chlorine,

her slit visible as she attempted star jumps in the pool
with me as her brace. I kissed my cracked lips to her elfin name.

Capturing the present seems so serious now,
the dust grows thick between gnawed ribs.

Beyond the Lion's Gate

I've been writing this tale for thirty eight years
as the brindled days flee like rabbits
through the holes in my jumper.
Left out in the English cold I flower
into a pale Elysian radiance.
The spring's clean taste I forgo,
the summer I close
with the shutters of an eye's wrinkle.
Someone will remember us
between ashen whispers,
someone will collect us after burning.
I will go first love
and whisper you a foolish tale in your sleep.
I'll look for you beyond the lion's gate.

Absence

I'm a man in badly fitting flesh,
it's too baggy in the leg,
this absence loiters in time.

Indigo Dreams Publishing
24 Forest Houses
Halwill
Beaworthy
Devon
EX21 5UU
www.indigodreams.co.uk